MYSTERIES OF THE MAYAN CALENDAR

Jim Pipe

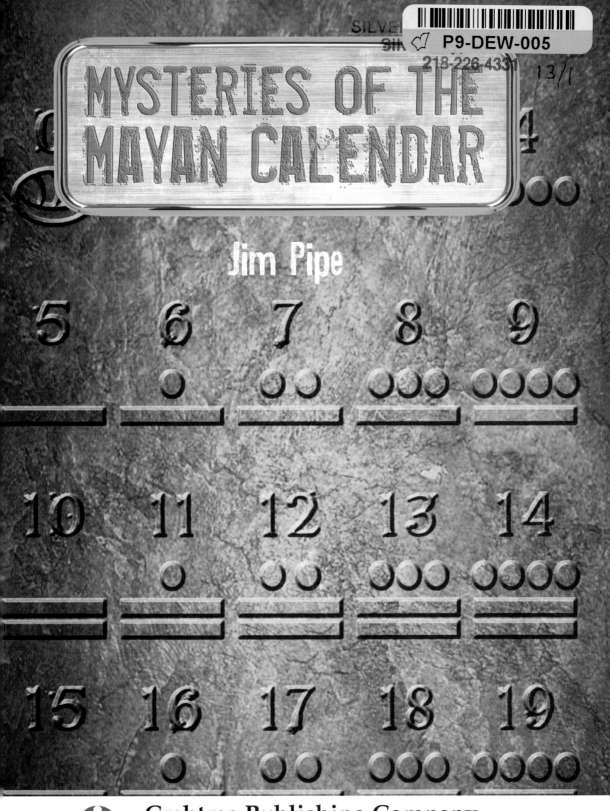

Crabtree Publishing Company
www.crabtreebooks.com

Crabtree Publishing Company

www.crabtreebooks.com

Author: Jim Pipe
Publishing plan research and development:
Sean Charlebois, Reagan Miller
Crabtree Publishing Company
Photo research: Sonya Newland
Editors: Sonya Newland, Kathy Middleton
Design: Tim Mayer (Mayer Media)
Cover design: Margaret Amy Salter
Production coordinator and prepress technician: Ken Wright
Print coordinator: Katherine Berti

Produced for Crabtree Publishing by
White-Thomson Publishing

Reading levels determined by
Publishing Solutions Group.
Content level: S
Readability level: N

Photographs:
Alamy: EPA/Tyrone Turner: pp. 6–7; David Cole: pp. 24–25; David Parker: p. 33; CarverMostardi: p. 34; Phototake Inc.: pp. 42–43; Corbis: Bettmann: pp. 22–23; Sandra Sebastian/epa: pp. 28–29; Historical Picture Archive: p. 39; Dreamstime: Vladimir Korostyshevskiy: p. 29; Getty Images: p. 15; Visuals Unlimited, Inc./Victor Habbick: pp. 1, 14; DEA/G. Dagli Orti: pp. 10, 30–31; AFP: p. 38; Bridgeman Art Library: pp. 44–45; NASA: NASA/SDO/ AIA: p. 37; NASA, ESA, and A. Schaller (for STScI): pp. 40–41; David A. Aguilar (CfA)/NASA ESA: p. 42; Shutterstock: front cover; Patryk Kosmider: pp. 3, 4, 18–19; f9photos: pp. 4–5, 12–13; Dave Rock: pp. 8–9; Jackson Gee: p. 11; sisqopote: pp. 16–17; Irafael: pp. 20, 21; Grigory Kubatyan: p. 25; sdecoret: pp. 26–27; oorka: pp. 32–33; Machkazu: pp. 34–35; zzoplanet: pp. 36–37; Welcomia: p. 40; Thinkstock: front cover.

J 529
PiP   H/LC   1/3/13

Library and Archives Canada Cataloguing in Publication

Pipe, Jim, 1966-
    Mysteries of the Mayan calendar / Jim Pipe.

(Crabtree chrome)
Includes index.
Issued also in electronic formats.
ISBN 978-0-7787-7932-2 (pbk.).--ISBN 978-0-7787-7923-0 (bound)

    1. Maya calendar--Juvenile literature. I. Title. II. Series:
Crabtree chrome

F1435.3.C14P56 2012   j529'.32978427   C2012-905537-9

Library of Congress Cataloging-in-Publication Data

Pipe, Jim, 1966-
    Mysteries of the Mayan calendar / Jim Pipe.
       p. cm. -- (Crabtree chrome)
    Includes index.
    ISBN 978-0-7787-7923-0 (reinforced library binding) --
ISBN 978-0-7787-7932-2 (pbk.) -- ISBN 978-1-4271-7855-8
(electronic pdf) -- ISBN 978-1-4271-7970-8 (electronic html)
    1. Maya calendar--Juvenile literature. 2. Maya astrology--
Juvenile literature. 3. Mayas--Prophecies--Juvenile literature.
I. Title.

    F1435.3.C14P57 2013
    529'.32978427--dc23
                                                   2012032203

Crabtree Publishing Company
www.crabtreebooks.com   1-800-387-7650

Printed in the U.S.A./112012/FA20121012

Published in Canada
Crabtree Publishing
616 Welland Ave.
St. Catharines, ON
L2M 5V6

Published in the United States
Crabtree Publishing
PMB 59051
350 Fifth Avenue, 59th Floor
New York, New York 10118

Published in the United Kingdom
Crabtree Publishing
Maritime House
Basin Road North, Hove
BN41 1WR

Published in Australia
Crabtree Publishing
3 Charles Street
Coburg North
VIC 3058

Contents

An Ancient Riddle

A Date with Destiny

December 21, 2012, marks the final date of the last known Mayan calendar. Did the Maya believe that the world would end on this date? There is no **evidence** for this, but not everyone was convinced.

▼ *Over 1,000 years ago, the Maya were a powerful people. Their incredible knowledge of the stars, science, and mathematics still fascinates us today.*

An Ancient Mystery

The Mayan calendar itself is like a giant puzzle. It is made up of several different calendars that fit together. We know how the Mayan calendar works, but not what it really means. People are still searching for clues to help solve this ancient mystery.

Thousands of people planned "Sacred Tours" to visit ancient Mayan ruins on this special date in the Mayan calendar.

evidence: proof that something has happened.

The Writing on the Wall

People have known about the Mayan calendar for hundreds of years. It is found in ancient books and in Mayan ruins. In 2011, **archeologists** made an amazing discovery in Guatemala, in the ruined Mayan city of Xultun. It was a wall of a house that looked like a blackboard. The wall was covered in numbers.

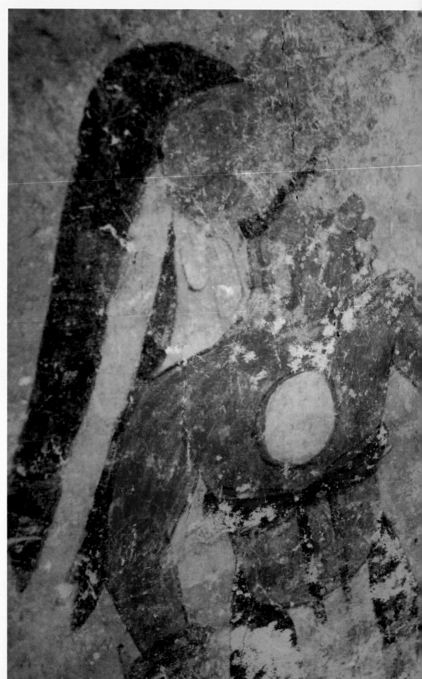

▶ *An archeologist cleans up a wall painting of a scribe at the ruined Mayan city of Xultun.*

Royal Scribblers

The numbers tracked how the Sun, the Moon, and the planets moved across the sky. The archeologists figured out the meaning of the numbers. This was a 13-year calendar, the earliest one ever found written on a Mayan wall. This discovery helped unlock the mystery of how the Mayan calendar worked.

Other paintings in the house at Xultun show a row of strange figures. The figures may be scribes, the people who wrote down the calendar.

archeologists: scientists who study ancient cultures.

The Mysterious Maya

Cities in the Forest

The search to uncover the mystery of the Mayan calendar begins in the thick, misty rain forests of Central America. Over 1,000 years ago, the Maya built great cities in what are now the countries of Mexico, Belize, and Guatemala.

▼ *This map shows the main areas where the Maya lived.*

Chichen Itza
Uxmal

Comalcalco
Tortuguero
Palenque
Xultun
Tikal
BELIZE

MEXICO

Izapa
GUATEMALA
Copán
HONDURAS

0   300 miles
0   300 kilometers

EL SALVADOR

Mayan Ruins

Many magnificent Mayan buildings and **pyramids** can still be seen. They stand in places such as Tikal, Palenque, Copán, and Uxmal. The Maya are still there, too. They are not a single people but many nations, sharing similar cultures, religions, and languages.

▼ *For hundreds of years, Mayan cities were lost in the jungles of Central America. Some may still be undiscovered.*

There are over 3,000 ruins in the ancient Mayan city of Tikal. Around 50,000 people may have lived there.

pyramids: solid shapes with four steep sides that meet at the top.

Mayan Beliefs

Paintings inside pyramids and in ancient books tell us about the Maya. They show holy **rituals** honoring the gods. The Maya believed there would be no crops without the help of the gods. They also thought their gods needed blood to grow strong. To feed the gods, Mayan priests killed enemies captured in battle.

▲ *These priests are cutting out a man's heart. More often they cut their own ear or nose to give blood to the gods.*

Fierce Gods

The carved heads of jaguars or eagles are found on many Mayan temples. These are probably two nature gods the Maya prayed to every day. Other gods were the God of Rain, Lady Rainbow, and the God of Sun. We do not know much about these Mayan gods.

Some Mayan ball games were a matter of life or death. Captured enemies were forced to play ball games. The Maya would cut off the head of the leader of the losing team. Sometimes entire teams were sacrificed to the gods!

▼ *This jaguar head is carved from stone. Mayan warriors also wore jaguar skins, teeth, and claws.*

rituals: holy ceremonies such as dancing, singing, and praying.

Palaces, Temples, and Tombs

The ancient Maya were also great builders. They built huge stone buildings such as palaces and temples. They buried their kings in large tombs. Most Maya were buried in their homes. This was so their relatives could still talk to them after they died.

Star Gazing

Mayan priests looked to the stars to guide them. The Maya were skilled **astronomers**. They tracked the movement of the Sun, stars, and planets to choose lucky dates and predict the future. They did not have telescopes, so they may have used pools of water to reflect the night sky.

◄ *The Pyramid of the Magician at Uxmal towers over the rain forest. Some Mayan pyramids are over 200 feet (60 meters) tall.*

To the ancient Maya, spotting the planet Venus in the morning meant it was a good day for a battle.

astronomers: scientists who study objects in space.

▲ *Mayan numbers were made up of bars and dots.*

Counting Time

The Maya were also very good at mathematics.
They counted by sets of 20 instead of 10 as we
do today. They could write large numbers using
just three symbols. These symbols stood for zero,
one, and five. Mayan astronomers used long
calculations to figure out their calendars.

Picture Writing

The Maya wrote down their history and what they saw in the sky in books called **codices**. These were made of soft tree bark. They folded like a fan. The Maya did not write using letters. Instead they used about 700 little symbols called glyphs.

▲ *This Mayan codex shows some of the symbols they used for writing*

The Dresden Codex is a famous Mayan book. Scientists still do not understand all the symbols in the codex. Could it hold the secrets of the Mayan calendar?

codices: old books made from sheets of paper, bark, or animal skin.

Two Calendars

One Mayan calendar, the Tzolk'in, counted 260 days and was used to determine holy days. Another, the Haab, was a **solar** calendar. It counted 365 days per year. The Haab was used in everyday life. Each day had its own sign linked to plants and animals.

Time to Hunt

Time was very important to the Maya. Each day was a god. He or she carried the world and passed it to another god the next day. One day might be good for hunting. Another could be good for planting crops. Being born on the right date was very important.

◀ *The Haab calendar had 18 months of 20 days, plus a short month of five days. These months are represented by the 19 glyphs in the circle.*

There were also five unlucky days, which had no names. The Maya believed this was a time when the gods might cause disaster.

solar: based on the cycle of the Sun.

Party Time!

The Maya **celebrated** events that happened every year. They also looked further ahead. Just once every 52 years, the Haab and Tzolk'in calendars ended at the same time. The Maya were happy to reach the end of this period safely. They celebrated with a big festival.

▼ *The Maya celebrated with music, singing, dancing, and fire.*

Rebirth

The festival was a time to make a fresh start. New layers were added to pyramids. Sometimes the Maya even lit huge bonfires to destroy their homes. Then they built them all over again.

In ancient times, most people died before they were 40 years old. If they lived past 52 years, the Maya believed they were born again.

celebrated: did something fun to mark an important date.

Looking to the Future

The Maya believed that calendars could help them **predict** the future. Mayan predictions often warned of bad harvests or wars. Other tribes of Central America have similar beliefs. They think the world is created and destroyed again and again.

Doom and Gloom

The Aztec people of Mexico believe the world has actually ended four times. Destroyed by jaguars, a storm, a volcano, and a great flood, the world started over again each time. But did the Maya really believe the world would end completely?

▼ *Mayan rulers waited for a good day to fight a battle. They believed the gods could help them win.*

▲ *Like the Tzolk'in calendar, the Aztec calendar counted 260 days a year.*

"Extraordinary claims require extraordinary evidence. Since the beginning of time there have been literally hundreds of thousands of predictions for the end of the world, and we're still here."

Astronomer Carl Sagan

predict: to work out what will happen in the future.

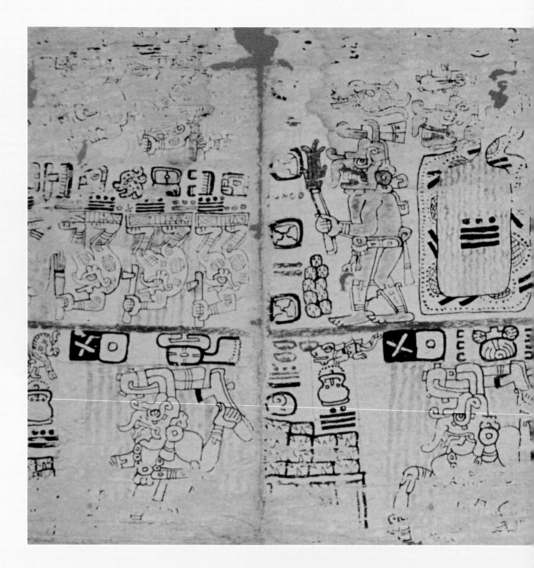

▲ *Only four ancient Mayan books survive.*
The Madrid Codex is one of them.

Clue 1: The Long Count

When people talk about the Mayan calendar, they actually mean a third calendar, called the Long Count. The other two Mayan calendars—the Haab and Tzolk'in—marked regular events but not the years. The Long Count recorded every day in history for thousands of years.

The Long Count appears in the books of *Chilam Balam*, which means the "jaguar priest." These books were written in the 1500s, long after the great Mayan cities disappeared.

How It Works

Each date in the Long Count calendar contained five numbers, for example, 4.5.4.3.1. Each number **represented** a grouping of a certain number of days. A mathematical calculation figured out how many days in total the date is from the beginning of the calendar.

represented: stood for

Doing the Math

The largest number that can be created using the Long Count is 13.0.0.0.0. This is the same as 1,872,000 days or 5,125 years. So we know how long the Long Count lasts. But when did it start?

▲ *The ancient Mayans carved their predictions in stone.*

Stone Pillars

The Maya carved important dates on tall stone pillars called **stelae**. Several stelae show that "Day 1" in the Mayan Long Count was August 11, 3114 B.C.E. on our calendar. Adding 1,872,000 days to this gives us an end date of December 21, 2012.

▲ *This stela stands in the ancient Mayan city of Copán.*

The Mayan rulers that appear on stelae often had strange names like "Smoke Monkey," "Fire-eating Serpent," and "Moon Jaguar."

stelae: tall slabs or stone pillars used to mark important events.

The End of Days

After 13.0.0.0.0 there are no more days in the Long Count. This means December 21, 2012 is the final date in the Long Count calendar. This is why some people believe that the Mayan calendar predicts the end of the world.

▲ *What can we expect on December 21, 2012?*

Back to the Future

Just because the calendar ends on this date, does not mean the Maya believed the world would end then. Most scientists think that the Long Count is more like the **odometer** in a car. If it ever reached 999,999 miles or kilometers, it would run out of numbers and simply go back to 0, starting all over again.

Our calendar is known as the Gregorian calendar. It was named after Pope Gregory XIII, who first used it in 1582. It repeats every 400 years.

odometer: a device that measures how far a car has traveled.

▲ *Modern Maya celebrate the start of a new year.*

Round and Round

We know that the Maya believed things happened in a particular order. This is called a **cycle**. The cycle repeated itself constantly. So the final date of 13.0.0.0.0 in the Long Count may just mean that the calendar goes back to 0.0.0.0.1. Then it starts again.

A Fresh Start

Today, when we reach the end of the year on December 31, we start a new year on January 1. For many modern Maya, starting the Long Count again is something to celebrate, too. They believe the whole world has a chance to make a fresh start.

The number 13.0.0.0.0 on the calendar may also be the date that the Maya believe the world was created.

▲ *It is more likely that the Mayan calendar represents a cycle of birth, death, and rebirth.*

cycle: a group of events that happen over and over again.

Written in Stone

Clue 2: Ancient Carvings

A strange stela was found in the ancient ruins at Tortuguero in Mexico. It describes something that is supposed to happen in 2012. This event involves Bolon Yokte. He was a Mayan god linked to both war and **creation**. The carving reads, "the god will come down from the sky."

▶ *Many Mayan gods were linked with destruction. The Maya believed that the Sun God Kinich Ahau sent his jaguars to Earth to eat humankind.*

"He Arrives"

Another carving found on a brick at Comalcalco in Mexico is just as puzzling. Talking about December 21, 2012, it simply says "He arrives." This carving was made about the same time as the one at Tortuguero. Perhaps they describe the same event.

The stela from Tortuguero is damaged, and some of the words are missing. People are only guessing that the rest of the story is about the end of the world.

creation: the beginning of the world.

Alien Invasion

The Swiss writer Erich von Däniken said that the "god from the sky" meant an alien invasion. He claimed that aliens built the pyramids in Egypt and Stonehenge in England. Could this be what the Mayan carving meant?

▶ *Lots of people say they have seen alien spaceships in the sky.*

They're Coming!

In the last 60 years, there have been many false alarms about alien invasion. A report in 2010 warned that three large spacecraft heading toward Earth would arrive in 2012. The report was a **fake**. The spaceships were just blobs of dust on the photograph.

▲ *Some crop circles look like Mayan designs.*

Sometimes strange shapes appear overnight in fields of crops. These flattened crops may look like landing sites for alien ships, but they are made by people using ropes and planks of wood as a joke.

fake: something that has been made up.

Clue 3: Stela 25

Another interesting Mayan carving comes from the ruins at Izapa in Mexico. Here, Stela 25 shows a bird on top of a large tree. One theory is that this represents the Sun lining up with the center of our **galaxy**, the Milky Way.

▲ *Several Mayan carvings show the World Tree, which archeologists think stood for the Milky Way.*

Cosmic Chaos

Some people believe this lining up will happen when the Long Count ends. They think it will cause terrible damage on Earth. There is no proof that the carving on Stela 25 really shows the Milky Way. Even if it does, we do not know that the Maya thought this meant the end of the world.

Every year in December, the Earth and Sun line up with the center of the Milky Way. There have been no harmful effects so far!

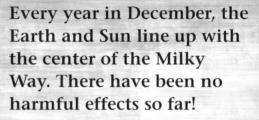

◄ *Our galaxy, the Milky Way, can be seen as a strip of stars and dust in the night sky.*

galaxy: a group of billions of stars, dust, and gas in space.

Planets in a Row

Like the Maya, some people still look at the night sky to tell the future. They suggest that on December 21, 2012, the planets will line up in a row. This might make the Sun wobble off center and tear itself apart.

Our Giant Sun

The pull between the planets and the Sun does make the Sun wobble, but only a little bit. This is because the Sun is so much bigger and heavier than the planets. It is more than 330,000 times bigger than Earth.

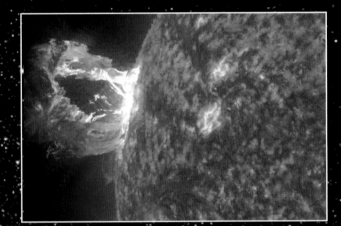

◄ *A huge solar flare shoots out of the Sun in April 2012.*

A giant **solar flare** could affect electricity on Earth, and even wipe out computer hard drives. This would be annoying, but not the end of the world!

solar flare: a bright burst on the Sun's surface.

Clue 4: The Dresden Codex

The Dresden Codex is a Mayan book. It contains calendars for different Mayan gods. It also contains tables about the Sun and the Moon. In the 1900s, the German scholar Ernst Forstemann pointed out that the last page of the codex showed a great flood.

▶ *The last page of the Dresden Codex shows a great flood coming from the mouth of a dragon.*

◀ *Many cultures around the world tell stories of ancient floods.*

Link to the Long Count

Many cultures have flood **myths** that tell of the end of the world. Is this what the Maya meant? The flood picture in the book does not show people being washed away. There is no link between the Dresden Codex and the end of the Long Count.

The Dresden Codex also includes the mysterious Serpent Number tables. These go back to 34,000 B.C.E., which does not tie in with the Long Count calendar.

myths: traditional stories.

Doomsday Stories

The Mayan calendar is still a mystery. No one knows if the Maya really predicted the end of the world. There are other doomsday stories, though. These have been inspired by the Mayan calendar, but most of them have nothing to do with the Maya.

◄ *If Planet X is real, this is what it would look like from the Moon.*

Beware Planet X

Some people say that a wandering planet, called
Niburu or Planet X, is heading toward Earth.
Perhaps the Maya saw it too. Astronomers have
found **dwarf planets** on the edge of our Solar
System. But none seems likely to crash into Earth.

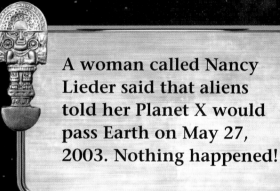

A woman called Nancy
Lieder said that aliens
told her Planet X would
pass Earth on May 27,
2003. Nothing happened!

▼ *The dwarf planet*
Xena was first spotted
in 2006.

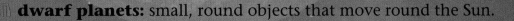

dwarf planets: small, round objects that move round the Sun.

Exploding Stars

Some people think that the end of the Mayan calendar is a warning that Earth will be wiped out by a supernova. A supernova is a very old star that explodes. This creates a giant wave of energy. The wave rushes through space at 68 million miles (110 million kilometers) per hour.

▼ *This huge bubble of gas is the remains of a supernova. Appearing over 400 years ago, it is the last supernova seen from Earth.*

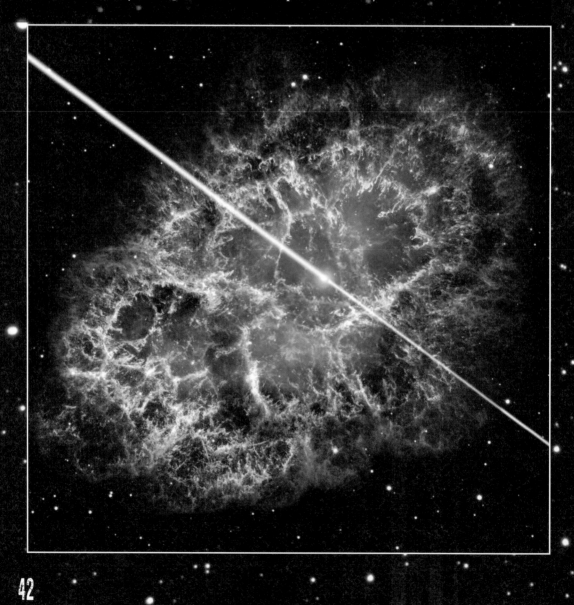

The Red Star

The red star Betelgeuse is set to explode in the next 100,000 years. No one knows exactly when it will happen. A supernova would need to be less than 50 **light years** away to threaten Earth, though. Betelgeuse is 640 light years away.

◀ *If Betelgeuse did explode, the only effect on Earth would be a very bright star in the night sky.*

"No star of that kind had ever shone before."

Astronomer Tycho Brahe, who saw a supernova in 1572

light year: how far light travels in a year, about six trillion miles.

The End of the Ancient Maya

The greatest mystery is what happened to the ancient Maya. Around 900 C.E., they suddenly stopped building. Their great cities became ruins. Many Maya may have been killed by disease. Some experts think the Maya could not grow enough food to survive.

The Modern Maya

Mayan people today still follow a calendar of 260 days. But they do not believe the world will end in December 2012. For them, this date just marks the end of a cycle. Life begins again afterward.

◀ *The Maya god Quetzalcoatl was the master of life.*

"The Mayan elders are angry with people who say the world will end in December 2012. The world will not end. It will be born again."

Carlos Barrios, a Mayan priest

 elders: important people in a tribe or family.

Learning More

Books

The Ancient Maya
by Jackie Maloy
(Children's Press, 2010)

You Wouldn't Want to Be a Mayan Soothsayer! Fortunes You'd Rather Not Tell
by Rupert Matthews
(Franklin Watts, 2007)

Amazing Maya Inventions You Can Build Yourself
by Sheri Bell-Rehwoldt
(Nomad Press, 2007)

In the Mayan Civilization
by Elizabeth Scholl
(Mitchell Lane Publishers, 2009)

Websites

www.history.com/topics/maya
Interesting videos from the History Channel.

http://history.howstuffworks.com/central-american-history/mayan-calendar.htm
Useful information about the Mayan calendar.

http://mayas.mrdonn.org/
Mayan daily life and legends.

www.kidskonnect.com/subject-index/16-history/256-ancient-mayan.html
Facts about the Ancient Mayan civilization

Glossary

archeologists Scientists who study ancient cultures

astronomers Scientists who study objects in space

celebrated Did something fun to mark an important date

codices Old books made from sheets of paper, bark, or animal skin

creation The beginning of the world

cycle A group of events that happen over and over again

dwarf planets Small, round objects that move around the Sun

elders Important people in a tribe or family

evidence Proof that something has happened

fake Something that has been made up

galaxy A group of billions of stars, dust, and gas in space

light year How far light travels in a year, about six trillion miles (10 trillion kilometers)

myths Traditional stories

odometer A device that measures how far a car has traveled

predict To work out what will happen in the future

pyramids Solid shapes with four steep sides that meet at the top

represented Stood for

rituals Holy ceremonies such as dancing, singing, and praying

solar Based on the cycle of the Sun

solar flare A bright burst on the Sun's surface

stelae Tall slabs or stone pillars used to mark important events

Index

Entries in **bold** refer to pictures